4-7-03   18.85   Regent   T

Sheryl Swoopes

Additional Titles in the Sports Reports Series

Roberto Alomar
Star Second Baseman
(0-7660-1079-1)

Charles Barkley
Star Forward
(0-89490-655-0)

Mark Brunell
Star Quarterback
(0-7660-1830-X)

Kobe Bryant
Star Guard
(0-7660-1828-8)

Terrell Davis
Star Running Back
(0-7660-1331-6)

Tim Duncan
Star Forward
(0-7660-1334-0)

Dale Earnhardt
Star Race Car Driver
(0-7660-1335-9)

Brett Favre
Star Quarterback
(0-7660-1332-4)

Kevin Garnett
Star Forward
(0-7660-1829-6)

Jeff Gordon
Star Race Car Driver
(0-7660-1083-X)

Wayne Gretzky
Star Center
(0-89490-930-4)

Ken Griffey, Jr.
Star Outfielder
(0-89490-802-2)

Scott Hamilton
Star Figure Skater
(0-7660-1236-0)

Anfernee Hardaway
Star Guard
(0-7660-1234-4)

Tim Hardaway
Star Guard
(0-7660-1500-9)

Grant Hill
Star Forward
(0-7660-1078-3)

Allen Iverson
Star Guard
(0-7660-1501-7)

Michael Jordan
Star Guard
(0-89490-482-5)

Shawn Kemp
Star Forward
(0-89490-929-0)

Jason Kidd
Star Guard
(0-7660-1333-2)

Michelle Kwan
Star Figure Skater
(0-7660-1504-1)

Tara Lipinski
Star Figure Skater
(0-7660-1505-X)

Mark Messier
Star Center
(0-89490-801-4)

Reggie Miller
Star Guard
(0-7660-1082-1)

Chris Mullin
Star Forward
(0-89490-486-8)

Hakeem Olajuwon
Star Center
(0-89490-803-0)

Shaquille O'Neal
Star Center
(0-89490-656-9)

Gary Payton
Star Guard
(0-7660-1330-8)

Scottie Pippen
Star Forward
(0-7660-1080-5)

Jerry Rice
Star Wide Receiver
(0-89490-928-2)

Cal Ripken, Jr.
Star Shortstop
(0-89490-485-X)

David Robinson
Star Center
(0-89490-483-3)

Barry Sanders
Star Running Back
(0-89490-484-1)

Deion Sanders
Star Athlete
(0-89490-652-6)

Junior Seau
Star Linebacker
(0-89490-800-6)

Emmitt Smith
Star Running Back
(0-89490-653-4)

Frank Thomas
Star First Baseman
(0-89490-659-3)

Chris Webber
Star Forward
(0-89490-799-9)

Tiger Woods
Star Golfer
(0-7660-1081-3)

Sheryl Swoopes

Star Forward

Ken Rappoport

Enslow Publishers, Inc.

40 Industrial Road	PO Box 38
Box 398	Aldershot
Berkeley Heights, NJ 07922	Hants GU12 6BP
USA	UK

http://www.enslow.com

For my dad, Jack Rappoport, who took me to my first
Brooklyn Dodgers game and sparked my love of sports.

Library of Congress Cataloging-in-Publication Data

Rappoport, Ken.
   Sheryl Swoopes, star forward / Ken Rappoport.
     p. cm. — (Sports reports)
   Includes bibliographical references (p.   ) and index.
   Summary: Presents the life and basketball career of this star player of the
Women's National Basketball Association.
   ISBN 0-7660-1827-X
   1. Swoopes, Sheryl—Juvenile literature. 2. Basketball players—United States—
Biography—Juvenile literature. 3. Women basketball players—United
States—Biography—Juvenile literature. [1. Swoopes, Sheryl. 2. Basketball players.
3. Women—Biography. 4. Afro-Americans—Biography.] I. Title. II. Series.
GV884.S88 R37   2002

796.323'092—dc21

                                                  2001007666

Printed in the United States of America

10 9 8 7 6 5 4 3 2 1

To Our Readers:
We have done our best to make sure that all Internet Addresses in this book were
active and appropriate when we went to press. However, the author and publisher
have no control over and assume no liability for the material available on those
Internet sites or on other Web sites they may link to. Any comments or suggestions
can be sent by e-mail to comments@enslow.com or to the address on the back cover.

Photo Credits: AP/Wide World Photos.

Cover Photo: AP/Wide World Photos.

Contents

Chapter 1

Breaking Through

Sheryl Swoopes, star forward of the Houston Comets, nervously waited for her chance. It was her first game in the Women's National Basketball Association (WNBA). She sat on the bench. In her second game, she also sat on the bench. The Olympic champion and college star found herself sitting on the bench again for her third game.

She had played only a few minutes in her first three games in the WNBA and did not look confident. What had happened to the great player who had led Texas Tech to the national collegiate championship? Where was the clutch performer who had led the United States Olympic women's basketball team to the gold medal? She was supposed to be one of the big stars in the new women's basketball league.

Swoopes was the first player signed by the WNBA for its first season in the summer of 1997. She had been one of the biggest sports personalities in the country after the U.S. women's basketball team took home the Olympic gold medal in 1996. Like Michael Jordan, she had her own brand of sneaker: "Air Swoopes." The WNBA was hoping her popularity would bring in fans.

But when the league opened for business, Sheryl Swoopes was missing. She had taken a leave of absence for six weeks to stay home with her new son, Jordan.

When she finally arrived in the WNBA late in the season, she appeared to be lost, unsure of herself. "When I first went out there, it was like, 'Oh, this is new. OK, I'm here now, what's going to happen?'" she said.[1]

Now it was game four for Sheryl Swoopes. But she was sitting on the bench, still waiting to get her first WNBA basket. Were her critics right? They said she was overweight and not ready. Maybe the critics were wrong. Maybe this would be the game when she finally broke out.

Cynthia Cooper had come out of practically nowhere to carry the Comets in Swoopes's absence.

Sheryl Swoopes worked hard to become a star in the WNBA. Here, Swoopes (22) drives past Tonya Edwards (13) of the Minnesota Lynx.

And the team had been winning. Cooper had played an exhausting game against Charlotte the previous night, scoring 39 points. Sheryl Swoopes wanted to help carry the scoring load.

"I thought that she might be tired and she could be double-teamed," Swoopes said of Cooper. "I knew if that was the case, then I would have to step up and pick up the slack."[2] So Swoopes prepared herself mentally to play the Utah Starzz.

Swoopes was off the bench and then it happened. She scored her first WNBA basket with 10:32 remaining in the first half of her fourth game and the crowd of some seven thousand people at Houston's Summit arena broke into thundering applause. "When I got the first basket, it was like a big burden had been lifted off my shoulders," she said. "I wanted to stop playing and start clapping myself. I thought that it would be enough just to be out there, but it wasn't. I had to score again to prove I could."[3]

And score again she did. Breaking loose from her defender, Swoopes put up a long shot from behind the three-point line. *Basket!* She found open space again and hit another three-pointer. Excitement was building. Sheryl Swoopes was in the flow of the game.

The Comets trailed, 12–5, when Swoopes made

FACT

If one word can describe Sheryl Swoopes, it is "winner." She has won championships in high school, in college, in the pros, and in the Olympics. Her overall total: a state high school championship, two college conference titles, an NCAA championship, two Olympic gold medals, a gold at the Goodwill Games, and four WNBA titles.

Sheryl Swoopes takes it to the hoop against Australia's Kristi Harrower during an Olympic Game in 2000. Despite getting off to a slow start as a pro, Swoopes is one of the greatest women's basketball players in the world.

her move. She scored 10 points in nine minutes to help her team take a 35–31 lead at the half. Here was the aggressive, confident Swoopes that everyone had expected. Gone was the player who had been unsure and unsteady in her first three games in the WNBA.

Sheryl Swoopes finished with 18 points in just 21 minutes of play. She added 6 rebounds and 2 assists as the Comets beat the Starzz, 76–56, for their fifth straight victory. The win tied the Comets with the New York Liberty for first place in the Eastern Conference race.

Sheryl Swoopes was back.

"Sheryl was a great help," said Cynthia Cooper. "When the Starzz double-teamed me, she got them off my back. The team has always felt that it was just a matter of time before she started to play like that. We just had to be patient with her, and she had to be patient with herself."[4]

Having patience had never been easy for Sheryl Swoopes. Ever since she was a little girl growing up in Texas, it seemed that she was always in a big hurry to make her mark.

Chapter 2

Big-Time Dreams

When Sheryl Swoopes was a young girl, all she wanted to do was join her older brothers' basketball games in the backyard. But they never wanted her to play. On this particular day, Sheryl was on the verge of tears.

She darted after the ball. But she was too little and her brothers were too fast. Her older brothers played "keep away"—keeping the ball away from Sheryl. Meanwhile, they continued to play their own game. They were busy sinking balls into their makeshift basket—an old bicycle wheel with the spokes punched out attached to a post. If Sheryl got too close, a shove moved her out of the way, or worse—sent her tumbling to the hard gravel court.

Sheryl ran crying into the house to her mother. She wanted her mom to comfort her. But her mom said, "Baby, I told you [that] you should stay in here with me."[1]

It was just the way things were when Sheryl was growing up in Brownfield, Texas. Brownfield is a small farming town in West Texas with a population of about 10,000 people. Sheryl Swoopes described Brownfield as "a very small town with lots of tumbleweeds."[2]

When Sheryl Swoopes was born on March 25, 1971, women's basketball had not yet gained the popularity that it enjoys today. There were fewer opportunities for women to play organized basketball, and no professional leagues like the WNBA.

Sheryl was about seven years old when she first showed a serious interest in basketball. Unfortunately, no one was taking her too seriously. "My mom didn't want me to play and my brothers didn't, either," Swoopes said. "But I was determined."[3]

Sheryl's brothers were unusually tough on her. "They never gave me the ball, they called me names and they told me I never was going to be any good. They thought I would quit."[4]

Her mom thought that might not be such a bad

Sheryl Swoopes is a driven player. Here she dribbles around defender Tracy Reid of the Charlotte Sting.

idea. She felt Sheryl should come into the house and play with her dolls. Sheryl's brothers played rough and her mother did not want her to get hurt. "But right from the beginning," Louise Swoopes said, "she wanted to prove that she could keep up with the boys."[5]

Soon Sheryl joined the Little Dribblers, a team in an all-girls recreational basketball league, and she was already ahead of the other players. Having played against her brothers in those rugged backyard games, Sheryl had no problem holding her own against girls of her own age. "They couldn't keep up with her," remembered her brother James.[6]

Sheryl and her three brothers were raised by their mother. Sheryl does not remember anything about her father. All she remembers is that times were tough when she was a young girl. "We grew up in a three-room house. Not three bedrooms. Three rooms."[7] Louise Swoopes worked at several jobs to support the family. Even so, Sheryl remembers, "We didn't have much money growing up and there were days when we didn't know where our next meal was coming from."[8]

They did know one thing, though: Sunday was church day. "I didn't have the pressures of alcohol and drugs. We were practically raised in a church."[9]

For a small-town girl, Sheryl had big-time dreams. She liked to read about faraway places and pictured herself as a flight attendant. She had seen such women on television and thought flying all over the world would be a glamorous and exciting career.

But it was only a dream. After all, how could she expect to get that kind of job without a college education? And where was the money for college going to come from? Sheryl thought she would be stuck in Brownfield for the rest of her life. That's what many people thought. "So many people told me that because I grew up in a single-parent home, I was never going to make anything of myself," Sheryl Swoopes said.[10]

Sheryl had other plans. She started to make a name for herself in high school basketball. The possibility of a college scholarship suddenly was within her reach. As a junior at Brownfield High School, it was already apparent that the five-foot ten-inch Swoopes was college basketball material. Her mother, who had once wanted her to play with dolls, and her brothers, who did not want her to play at all, now were her biggest fans. Many college scouts crowded around to see her play.

With Swoopes leading the way in her junior year of high school, Brownfield became a power in its

FACT

Sheryl Swoopes was only a high school sophomore when she was named to the Texas All-State basketball team. By the time she was a senior at Brownfield High, she had the added award of Female High School Player of the Year in the state. Other honors and awards in her senior year: selection to three All-American teams in 1989 and the MVP of the Texas High School Girls Coaches Association North-South All-Star Game.

own territory. Now it was on the verge of winning the Texas State Championship in Class 3A at the 1988 tournament in Austin.

The Lady Cubs' job would not be easy. They beat Ingleside in the semifinals of the girls University Interscholastic League State Basketball Tournament. Then they faced powerful Hardin-Jefferson for the championship. Hardin-Jefferson had charged into the finals with a powerful team. In fact, no one had beaten the Lady Hawks in 34 games that season.

After three quarters, Hardin-Jefferson led, 31–27. It was Sheryl Swoopes's time to shine. She scored basket after basket to help Brownfield take a 41–36 lead with 3:34 left in the game. Back came Hardin-Jefferson to cut Brownfield's lead to 41–40. But then Swoopes hit two free throws as the Lady Cubs held off their opponents. Swoopes had done it all for Brownfield. When the game was over, she had 26 points and 18 rebounds. And the Lady Cubs had done the seemingly impossible, beating Hardin-Jefferson, 49–40. The performance established a reputation for Swoopes as a clutch player, something that would carry throughout her professional career.

Swoopes was the Female Player of the Year in Texas as a senior. Offers poured in from colleges

Sheryl Swoopes (7) controls the ball while being guarded by Australia's Robin Maher (4) during a game from the 1996 Olympics.

around the country. Sheryl picked the one that seemed to be the right choice. She chose the University of Texas at Austin, the big school with the biggest basketball reputation in the state.

It made sense for everyone—everyone, that is, but Sheryl Swoopes.

Chapter 3

Small-Town Girl, Big-Time Player

The phone rang in the office of South Plains College women's basketball coach Lyndon Hardin. An ordinary day was about to turn extraordinary. At the other end of the line was Sheryl Swoopes, one of the most sought-after female high school basketball players in Texas. She was asking if he had a place for her on his team. It was unbelievable.

Swoopes had already announced her intention to play for the University of Texas. The Longhorns were big time. Their sports program overshadowed everyone else's in the state. They had offered Swoopes four years of free schooling and plenty of television exposure. South Plains was just a small junior college in Levelland, Texas. It was hardly known outside of the West Texas area. People who attend junior colleges go for only two years. Then they can move on to a four-year school—like the University of Texas.

Hardin was not the only one surprised by Swoopes's request for a spot on his team. Texas was a nationally ranked women's basketball power. People who followed the sport were also stunned by her decision to play for a junior college team. Friends told her she had lost the opportunity to be a college All-American.

But South Plains had something that the University of Texas did not have—location. The school was close to Sheryl's hometown of Brownfield. After traveling 400 miles to visit the University of Texas, Sheryl felt homesick.

"Texas was the only school I really considered out of high school," Swoopes said. "It was a big national basketball power and I thought they could take my game to another level. But once I got there. . . well, I just didn't realize how far it was from home."[1]

Swoopes never unpacked. Less than a week later, she was back in Brownfield.

"Mama, I just don't want to go back there [University of Texas]," Swoopes told her mother, Louise.

Sheryl Swoopes battles Mwadi Mabika of the Los Angeles Sparks for a loose ball.

"Well, then, you don't have to," her mother said.[2]

Desperate for Swoopes to return, Texas coach Jody Conradt phoned her several times. Would she change her mind? No luck. "This is the kind of thing you dread every fall," Conradt said.[3]

Sheryl had called Coach Hardin on a Sunday morning. He told her if she really wanted to play for South Plains, she should be at the school at 8:00 a.m. on Monday. She was there at 7:30.

Conradt's loss was Hardin's gain. Hardin was an experienced coach, but he had never coached a player of Swoopes's all-around ability. At six feet, Swoopes did not especially enjoy a height advantage over other players. Most of the players in women's college basketball were as tall, many even taller. Her high dribbling technique was less than perfect. It seemed she was an easy target for steals. But she was far too quick for her opponents. Conradt thought Swoopes had a perfect blend of size, speed, and quickness. "She's so effective offensively because she doesn't need any help, once she has the ball. She just creates shots."[4]

Her standard operating procedure would go something like this:

> Swoopes comes up court with the ball, walking stiffly upright, almost mechanically. Her high dribble gives the impression that it would be

easy to take the ball away from her. Good luck. All of a sudden, Swoopes roars by the player guarding her, leaving her opponent flatfooted. There is another defender, this one taller. She steps in front of Swoopes as she darts toward the basket. Swoopes pulls up, soars into the air and fires over her opponent with the quickest release in women's basketball. Score!

Sheryl Swoopes was just as outstanding on the other side of the ball. Many an opposing player was left embarrassed, and empty-handed, after having the ball stripped away by the lightning-quick Swoopes.

She was a player who felt comfortable at any position, and very often played them all. If someone was

FACT

In two seasons at South Plains College, Sheryl Swoopes set fifteen school records. Among them:

Most points in a career 1,554

Best career scoring average 25.4

Most points in a game 45

Most rebounds in a career 705

Most rebounds in a game 22

Best career rebound average 11.5

needed to post up under the basket, Swoopes was there. (She had primarily played center in high school.) She could also drive to the basket for a layup like a guard, or pick off rebounds like a forward. Shooting three-pointers from long range like a shooting guard was also no problem. And setting up teammates for baskets like a point guard was her game, too. "She makes everything look easy," said Hardin, who usually used Swoopes as both a forward and a center.[5]

Hardin expected big things from Swoopes at South Plains. He did not have to wait long. Early in her first season, she scored a school-record 45 points in one game. It was one of fifteen records she would establish at the school. In her two seasons at South Plains, she helped the Lady Texans win 52 of 64 games and a regional championship. In 1991, at the end of her second season at South Plains, Swoopes was selected as the female National Junior College Player of the Year. That went along with All-American recognition for the second straight year—the only two-time All-American that South Plains ever had.

Swoopes was thankful for the opportunity to play at South Plains. She did not regret it for a minute. "I really learned what basketball is all about," Swoopes said. "It prepared me for Division I classes and Division I basketball."[6]

Next stop: Texas Tech.

Sheryl Swoopes could have gone to DePaul, Oklahoma, or Western Kentucky. But she chose Texas Tech. Once again, she wanted to stay close to home. Texas Tech coach Marsha Sharp knew Swoopes would give the Red Raiders' program an immediate boost. Maybe she would bring them a Southwest Conference (SWC) title. Maybe she could even bring them their first national championship.

Texas Tech's Lady Raiders had been to the SWC Finals on five previous occasions. Each time they lost to archrival Texas. The all-time series between the teams was not even close. Texas had dominated thoroughly, winning 37 straight games until Texas Tech finally managed a two-point victory in the SWC tournament in 1991. Texas Tech had never even beaten Texas on its own home court—a streak that extended back fifteen seasons. Now with Swoopes in the lineup, Texas Tech fans were hoping that things would change. Beating Texas would be a major step for the Lady Raiders in their quest for respect.

On a January night in 1992, fans filled Municipal Coliseum in Lubbock, Texas, to watch the Lady Raiders host the Lady Longhorns. There was a buzz

Sheryl Swoopes reacts after nailing a three-point shot.

in the air, the game taking on the atmosphere of a postseason playoff contest. The largest crowd ever to see a Lady Raiders game—some fifty six hundred people—would be watching. Fans held posters that read "BEAT TEXAS!" As usual, Texas was ranked in the Top 25—as it had been for 170 straight weeks dating back several seasons. Texas Tech had yet to make the Top 25 in the 1991–92 season.

The crowd cheered as the Lady Raiders took the court. Fans gave special attention to Sheryl Swoopes, as usual. SWOOOOOOOOOOPES! The sound of the fans prolonging the double-O in her name came down from the very top of the arena and seemed to fill every seat and every corner. It had become a familiar salute to Swoopes, usually after

FACT

Sheryl Swoopes was named the National Junior College Player of the Year in 1991. Other honors while playing at South Plains College:

NJCAA All-American, 1989–90, 1990–91

Kodak All-American, 1989–90, 1990–91

Western Junior College Conference MVP, 1990–1991 and co-MVP in 1989–90 she scored a basket. It had taken Sheryl a little while to get used to it. "I thought our fans were booing me at first," she said.[7]

Against Texas, the baskets began adding up for Swoopes. So did the chants. Black and red streamers came floating out of the stands and filled the court.

The Lady Raiders' attack centered around Swoopes. And it was no wonder. She was hitting every imaginable shot from the floor, some of them uncontested. Layups, short jumpers, and shots off rebounds all turned into scores. In all, she made 14 of 21 shots and scored 32 points. The final score was Texas Tech 78, Texas 65.

It was only the second time in 39 games that Coach Conradt's Texas team had lost to Texas Tech. It was doubly painful for Conradt, who had recruited Swoopes as a freshman only to lose her. "I knew I should have kidnapped her when I had the chance," Conradt said jokingly.[8]

Coach Conradt had to be thinking the same thing again when Swoopes exploded for another big game against Texas in the SWC Tournament Finals. Swoopes had won the honor of SWC Player of the Year. Now she showed why, leading Texas Tech to its first conference championship with a 76–74 victory over Texas. The Lady Raiders, who had also won the regular season championship, became the

Sheryl Swoopes (22) battles Teresa Weatherspoon (11) for a loose ball.

first women's team besides Texas and Arkansas to win the SWC Tournament.

With Swoopes leading the way, the Lady Raiders had reached just about all their goals. But they still had not won a national championship. They had beaten Texas, cracked the Top 25, and won the SWC Tournament. Now with Swoopes coming back for her senior year in 1992–93, only one goal remained: the national title.

Chapter 4

A Special Season

On a cold night in Lubbock, Texas, thousands of fans waited in line in subfreezing temperatures for hours. They were there to buy tickets for Sheryl Swoopes's final home game. Few college players—men or women—had captured the imagination of the public like Sheryl Swoopes had in her senior year at Texas Tech.

She could not walk anywhere on the Texas Tech campus without being asked for an autograph. Game after game, large crowds at Texas Tech turned out to watch the popular player, chanting "Swoooooooopes" every time she made a big basket or a big play.

Actually, it did not matter where the games were

played. Swoopes was drawing attention all over the country, making the Lady Raiders one of the most-watched teams in America. On January 2, 1993, Swoopes scored a school and Southwestern Conference record 48 points against Washington in a big intersectional battle.

At South Plains College, Swoopes had led the Lady Texans to their first regional championship. Now she was attempting to lead the Lady Raiders to their first national title. She had help from the other players on the team. Texas Tech featured a string of good players including Krista Kirkland, Cynthia Clinger, Noel Johnson, Stephanie Scott, Janice Farris, and Michi Atkins. They were part of a group of home-grown talent at Texas Tech, featuring eleven of twelve players from Texas. In fact, nine of them were from West Texas just like Swoopes.

At the start of the 1992–93 season, the Lady Raiders were regarded as one of the top women's teams in college basketball. Just to be among the best was no small accomplishment. It was a field crowded with great individual players and great teams, including defending NCAA champion Stanford and perennial contender Tennessee. In addition, the strong University of Texas team was in Texas Tech's own conference. The Lady Raiders went into the season ranked No. 15 in the country.

Stanford, with all five starters back, was the favorite to win another national championship.

Sheryl Swoopes scored a career-high 35 points in the season-opening game at Stanford. Although Texas Tech lost to the Cardinals, the Lady Raiders showed a lot of courage with a great second-half rally behind Swoopes, who hit all eleven of her shots. Despite losing, the Lady Raiders had also shown coach Marsha Sharp something encouraging. "The first game of the year, playing on their court, that we had enough courage to stay in the game pleases me," she said.[1]

She had to be even more pleased as the season went on. The Lady Raiders were piling up victory after victory. Highlights of the regular season included triumphs over Louisiana Tech and Miami, two of the nation's ranked teams.

The year also included a personal honor that thrilled Swoopes: South Plains College was retiring her jersey number. It was the first time in its history that the junior college had retired an athlete's number. A big crowd was on hand for "Sheryl Swoopes Day" at the Texas Dome in Levelland. Usually calm and controlled, Swoopes suddenly lost her composure during the ceremonies. "Actually, I didn't expect that many people to come," she said. "When

Sheryl Swoopes (22) of Texas Tech prepares to launch a jump shot against Vanderbilt.

people started filtering in, I had tears in my eyes. It brought back so many memories."[2]

Her main focus, though, was on winning a national championship for Texas Tech. "When I went to Tech, people in Brownfield said Tech could never get to the Final Four," Swoopes said. "I want my teammates and I to go more than anything."[3]

Going into the Southwest Conference playoffs, the Lady Raiders were playing their best basketball of the season. The same could be said of Swoopes.

In a late-season game against Texas, she scored 37 points to give Texas Tech its first victory ever at Austin. The teams seemed destined to meet for a second straight year in the SWC Finals. The two SWC powerhouses had split the season series 1–1, each team winning on the other's home court.

As expected, it was Texas Tech vs. Texas in the finals. Unexpectedly, Sheryl Swoopes had a horrible start, missing six of her first seven shots. The Lady Raiders fell behind, 26–11. But her teammates kept feeding her the ball, confident that she would come through as she always had for them. "I don't even think about her having a bad night," Texas Tech Coach Marsha Sharp said. "When we had a timeout, I looked at her face and I knew we would be OK. She still had that look that, 'We're going to make this

FACT

Most athletes are lucky to have their jersey retired once. It has happened to Sheryl Swoopes twice—at South Plains College and at Texas Tech. Her number both times was 22.

happen.' The bigger the game, the more you get that look that, 'I'm not going to be denied.'"[4]

Amazingly, Swoopes ended up scoring 53 points in a 78–71 victory for Texas Tech. Talk about a one-woman team. Swoopes had more than doubled the entire combined scoring output of her teammates! Maybe it was just playing the Lady Longhorns that brought out the best in her. Swoopes made no secret of her pleasure at beating Texas. It was the big school in the state and Texas Tech's archrival. For Sheryl, it was also personal. It was the school she had left behind as a homesick college freshman—the school that was too big and too far away from her loved ones. "I have nothing against Texas now," she said, "but I always want to do a little better against Texas than anyone else."[5]

Whether facing Texas or another team, Sheryl Swoopes was usually the game's best player. She rarely had an off night during the 1992–93 season. She loved to dribble the length of the court to the area of the free-throw line, pull up and shoot a jump shot. Opposing teams knew she was going to do it, yet were usually defenseless to stop her.

Speed was a big part of Sheryl Swoopes's game. Against full-court pressure, she often simply outran the defense the length of the court to score a layup. She was strong in all facets of the game. She was

Texas Tech's Sheryl Swoopes works out of a tight spot during the 1993 NCAA Championship Game.

usually among the top rebounders and defensive players. It was no surprise that Swoopes was named the National Player of the Year and the SWC Player of the Year.

It was on to the NCAA Tournament and a meeting with Washington. Lubbock Municipal Coliseum was packed. Some eighty-five hundred fans—400 over capacity—crowded into the arena to watch Swoopes's final home game as a Lady Raider. They serenaded her one last time with the now familiar "Swoooooooopes" chant. She scored 30 points to lead Texas Tech to victory.

Next up was Southern Cal. Again, no problem with Swoopes scoring 33. That put the Lady Raiders among the final eight teams in the NCAA Tournament for the first time in their history. Said USC coach Marianne Stanley, "[Swoopes] has that mental toughness great offensive players need. She sees all kinds of tough defenses, but she has the mental toughness to overcome them."[6]

Prior to meeting Texas Tech in the West Regional finals, Colorado coach Ceal Barry was asked the key question: How did Colorado plan to stop Sheryl Swoopes? "No one matches up with Sheryl Swoopes," Barry said.[7]

She was right. Colorado had no answers for Swoopes, who scored 36 to lead Texas into the Final

FACT

The 1993 NCAA playoffs were a showcase event for Sheryl Swoopes. Her 47 points broke the women's record by 19. Dawn Staley of Virginia and Dena Head of Tennessee shared the previous record with 28. It was also the most points by a player (man or woman) in the NCAA title game, bettering Bill Walton's 44 for UCLA in 1973.

Four. The Lady Raiders were now two victories away from their first national championship. Teammates and opponents alike were praising Swoopes. "We used to call Sheryl the Michael Jordan of women's basketball," said Johnson. "Now we call Michael Jordan the Sheryl Swoopes of men's basketball."[8]

Texas Tech was not the only newcomer to the Final Four field. Vanderbilt had finished the regular season as the nation's No. 1 team. They were among the first-timers along with Big Ten powers Ohio State and Iowa. Stanford and Tennessee, the preseason favorites, along with powerhouse Virginia, had all been upset in the playoffs.

Texas Tech had the tough job of playing Vanderbilt and its imposing six-foot ten-inch center, Heidi Gillingham. Could the Lady Raiders beat the Commodores? It was no contest. Swoopes had her hand in every part of the game, including a key steal and two free throws in the final nine minutes. She propelled the Lady Raiders to a 60–46 victory over the nation's No. 1-ranked team. Texas Tech was on its way to the national championship game.

The Lady Raiders would face Ohio State, which had beaten Iowa in the other semifinal game. "For Ohio State, the answer to winning is simple," said one sports writer. "Stop Sheryl Swoopes.

Accomplishing that feat isn't so simple."[9] Swoopes had scored 31 points against Vanderbilt and needed just five more points to break the five-game tournament record of 134 set by Tennessee's Bridgette Gordon in 1989.

It would seem to be hard for even Swoopes to top her performances in the previous four NCAA playoff games. No team had been able to keep her under 30 points. She had done just about everything for her team against the toughest competition in the nation. Now the Lady Raiders would need Swoopes at her very best against Ohio State. It would be the biggest game of her career and her school's history. It was not likely that Texas Tech would be able to dominate Ohio State. After all, Ohio State had beaten top-ranked Vanderbilt in the semifinals. But no one was betting against them in the championship finals.

The Lady Raiders' rise among college basketball's elite throughout the season had been an amazing story. At the start of the year, the Lady Raiders had not even been picked to win their own conference. Now they were in the NCAA Finals. Despite Swoopes, the Lady Raiders were pretty much an unknown quantity among the top teams.

That changed as quickly as Swoopes took the court against Ohio State in the finals. Sixteen thousand people watched at the Omni Center in Atlanta

Sheryl Swoopes is defended by Ohio State's Nikki Keyton during the 1993 NCAA Championship Game.

along with a national television audience. Sheryl Swoopes made everyone sit up and take notice. She scored 23 points in the first half to help the Lady Raiders take a 40–31 lead. But it was far from over. Back came Ohio State behind Katie Smith, who scored 20 points in the second half. Three times the Buckeyes took a one-point lead, the last with just 8:30 left in the game. This was championship game pressure at its most intense.

The final minutes turned into an all-out shooting war between two explosive teams. It was still anybody's game. Five times, Ohio State pulled within two points of Texas Tech in the final six minutes.

As the team leader, Sheryl Swoopes stepped forward time and again with key shots. "Whenever [the Buckeyes] got within two or three, I decided to take control of the game," Swoopes said.[10]

With 2:16 remaining in the game, Ohio State pulled within two to make the score 75–73. It was still anybody's game. Finally, it was Sheryl Swoopes's game. She hit two free throws with two minutes left for a 77–73 Texas Tech lead. Then with just under a minute left, she drove the lane and went up for a basket. She was fouled, and made the shot. Now Texas Tech had a seven-point lead. It was enough of a cushion for the Lady Raiders to

FACT

Until Sheryl Swoopes arrived, Texas Tech had never won the national championship in women's basketball. In her two years with the Lady Raiders, Texas Tech won the national title and two Southwest Conference titles. Texas Tech's overall record with Swoopes: 58–8.

withstand a late rally by Ohio State. The final score was Texas Tech 84, Ohio State 82.

With a staggering 47 points, Sheryl Swoopes had become the player of the moment for Texas Tech and a player for the ages in college basketball. Her point total was the most ever scored in an NCAA championship game, by either a man or a woman.

"At first I couldn't believe it was over," Swoopes said. "I was thinking, 'Is this real? Have we really done it?' Then [backup guard] Melinda White ran up and pinched me and I knew it was real."[11]

Swoopes, tears flowing, walked over to Krista Kirkland, another key player in the Lady Raiders' run to the championship. They embraced. It was a personal moment for both of them. Swoopes felt Kirkland had played a subpar game in Texas Tech's upset of Vanderbilt in the semifinals. She had challenged Kirkland to play a better game in the finals. Kirkland responded with a solid all-around performance. The Lady Raiders also got some key plays from Clinger, Atkins, Scott, and Johnson to help point them in the right direction.

But Sheryl Swoopes stood head and shoulders above everyone in the eyes of Ohio State coach Nancy Darsch. "She hurt us, not just by the scoring," Darsch said of Swoopes, who received the Outstanding Player Award in the tournament. "I

*Sheryl Swoopes celebrates on the court after helping Texas Tech win
the Women's NCAA Division 1 basketball title on April 4, 1993.*

saw us get a little down, a little dejected, when she scored some tough shots against us."[12]

The Texas Tech players continued to rejoice for what seemed like endless moments on the court. Many climbed into the stands to be with family members. Sheryl Swoopes's mother, Louise, had made a nineteen-hour car ride from Brownfield, Texas, to Atlanta, Georgia, to watch her daughter in action.

Many still could not believe they had won the championship. "Everybody had doubts at the beginning of the season," Stephanie Scott said. "Even we did."[13] But no team in the country had played as well as Texas Tech, particularly in the second half of the season. The Lady Raiders had won their last nineteen games and Swoopes had finished her college career in style.

Sheryl Swoopes was an All-American. She was also the Women's College Basketball Player of the Year, and she won the Outstanding Player Award in the NCAA playoffs. Best of all, she was finally a national champion. Sheryl Swoopes had proved wrong critics who had said she could not be an All-American at Texas Tech and could not win a national championship there.

Amazingly, she had done it all. And now all she had to do was figure out what to do with the rest of her life.

Chapter 5

Going for the Gold

Sheryl Swoopes versus Michael Jordan? Yes. It had started as a friendly game of one-on-one. Suddenly, it was a nationally televised event.

Swoopes had caught the nation's attention by helping to win the NCAA championship at Texas Tech. Now she was again in the spotlight.

Michael Jordan had invited Swoopes to assist him at his basketball camp in Chicago during the summer of 1993. One day, they were talking and Jordan issued a challenge. "A lot of people say you're the female Michael Jordan," he said. "Get out here and show me what you've got."[1]

Before she knew it, Sheryl Swoopes was playing one-on-one with the player that she admired the most. She showed Michael Jordan plenty, hitting the first three shots. Back came Jordan. He drove past Swoopes, slapping away her hand-check to score a layup. He scored on three-pointers from long range. It was down and dirty playground basketball— complete with trash talk, dares, and charges of "cheating"—all in good fun. Jordan eventually won, 7–4. But he had been tested by the hard-driving Swoopes.

"Girl, you can play," Jordan told Swoopes after the game. "I watched you play and you did some things that kind of reminded me of myself."[2]

Parts of the contest were shown on national television later in the year.

With her brilliant performance in the 1993 NCAA Finals, Sheryl Swoopes had become one of the best-known female basketball players in America. Some called her the best in the world.

There had been stories about her in national magazines and newspapers. There were even television appearances. "Swoopes—as in hoops," was a commonly used expression whenever the media wrote about Sheryl Swoopes. Her fame, flashy play, and good looks led to a shoe contract with Nike. She had her own line of sneakers called "Air Swoopes." It was a first for a female basketball player.

Playing against Michael Jordan was one thing.

But Sheryl Swoopes missed playing basketball on a regular basis. When she finished college she had her sights set on the Olympics, but that was still three years away.

There were no professional leagues for women in America at that time, so Sheryl Swoopes traveled all the way to Italy to play for a team called Basket Bari. She was back sooner than expected, though. "They reneged on their part of the contract," Swoopes said. "I was supposed to have an apartment and a car. When I got the apartment, they never put a phone in it, so I couldn't call home. They didn't pay me. Things like that."[3]

After just ten games in Italy, she came back to the United States. She kept in condition by practicing with the Texas Tech team. There was no lack of basketball work. The United States National Team called. Could Swoopes play in the 1994 Goodwill Games? Next thing she knew, she added a gold medal to her collection of trophies.

It was an important experience for Sheryl Swoopes in other ways. Her lack of international exposure had put her behind other prominent players. "She kind of learned that summer what she needed to work on and just how physical the [international] games were," said Tara VanDerveer, who coached Swoopes at the Goodwill Games.[4]

Teammates on the 1996 U.S. Women's Olympic basketball team, from left to right: Venus Lacey, Sheryl Swoopes, and Lisa Leslie.

Swoopes weighed only 145 pounds. She was really too small to handle the rough physical style of international play. So she did something about it when the call came for the 1995 United States National Team. She lifted weights to prepare herself for the 1996 Olympics.

For Swoopes, just making the United States National Team had been a thrill and the brilliant end to a long, hard struggle. Her first try for the Olympic Team in 1992 ended in disappointment when she injured her knee and needed surgery. She vowed that next time would be different.

Some were calling the 1996 U.S. Olympic Team the greatest collection of talent in women's basketball history.

Women's college basketball in America had been helped by television exposure. It had gone on to reach new levels in recent years. Swoopes was among many popular college stars, including Rebecca Lobo (Connecticut), Lisa Leslie (Southern Cal), and Theresa Edwards (Georgia), featured on the 1996 Olympic Team. It was a veteran team with plenty of international experience, led by Edwards' three previous Olympic appearances.

It was also a team of great determination. The American women hungered for the gold medal. They had so far failed to win it at the 1991 Pan-Am

Games, the 1992 Barcelona Olympics, and the 1994 World Championships.

In the past, the Americans did not have much time to train or play together. This time would be different. The ambitious Americans practiced for nearly a year before the Olympics. They played 52 exhibition games on four continents, in nine different countries. Along the way, they received plenty of attention. Coach VanDerveer said it was like traveling with a group of rock stars.

It was a trip worth remembering for Sheryl Swoopes. As a freshman in college, she had left the University of Texas because 400 miles was too far from home. Now she was traveling thousands of miles away from her mom and husband, Eric Jackson, to follow a dream. (Swoopes had met Jackson in high school. The two were married in 1995.)

The tour experience toughened her as a player and sharpened her skills. Swoopes said she was surrounded by women who were "just as good as I am, if not better. That means that every time I step out on the court I've got to take my game to a different level."[5]

The American women turned the exhibition schedule into their own personal victory tour. At the end of it, they had won every game and were among

Sheryl Swoopes (7) battles beneath the basket for a rebound.

the favorites to capture the gold medal at the Olympics. Swoopes appeared on the *David Letterman* and *Jay Leno* shows, and the team was featured on the cover of *Sports Illustrated*. Not even in her wildest dreams could Sheryl Swoopes have imagined it.

On its exhibition tour, the United States National Team had beaten each team it played against. Many of those teams were scheduled to compete in the Olympics.

The Brazilians had upset the Americans in the 1994 World Championships. It would be great if the women of the United States could play the Brazilians in another gold medal game and beat them. But the American team could not afford to look that far ahead.

"The public, when they see that [52–0] record, they think, 'We know you're definitely going to win the gold,'" Swoopes said. "They think that simply because we've played some of the teams that we're going to play in Atlanta [the Olympics], that means we're going to roll over them."[6]

The American women knew it would be tough to go undefeated in the Olympics. It was not an exhibition tour. It was the real thing.

In their opening Olympic game, Cuba came close to beating the Americans. Even though it had beaten

FACT

Sheryl Swoopes is a junk food addict. According to the Houston Comets' media guide, she took $200 worth of snacks with her when she traveled to Siberia with the touring USA Basketball Women's National Team before the 1996 Olympics.

the Cubans six straight times, the United States team trailed 20–13 before rallying to take the lead. The Americans pulled away at the end for a 101–84 victory.

Next up for the United States women was the team from the Ukraine. Swoopes had a solid all-around game with 11 points, 7 assists, and 6 rebounds as the Americans won. Despite the ease of victory, Coach VanDerveer felt her team had to play better to win a gold medal. Two days later, against Zaire, the Americans won by 60 points—the most lopsided victory in Olympic history.

Then terror struck at the Olympics. A pipe bomb went off in Centennial Olympic Park, killing two people and wounding 111 others. Sports had now taken a backseat. The International Olympic Committee (IOC) met to decide whether to continue the games. The blast sparked more bomb threats, one of them at the Georgia Dome where the United States women's basketball team was supposed to play.

The IOC decided the games would continue and Sheryl Swoopes and her teammates agreed with the decision. "We were not going to let this one idiot say, 'Look, I'm going to do this, I'm going to draw all the attention away from the athletes and make you guys want to go home,' or whatever."[7]

Swoopes (right) embraces teammate Ruthie Bolton after the U.S. women's team wins the 1996 Olympic gold medal by defeating Brazil, 111–87.

Security was tightened at every Olympic event. Authorities were on the alert for anyone or anything suspicious. Fans entering the arena for the United States versus Australia women's basketball game found the mood more somber. The game opened with a moment of silence for the bombing victims and their families.

This was not an easy game for the Americans. Australia led by as many as six points in the first half and was only two points behind the Americans with less than sixteen minutes to play. Enter Sheryl Swoopes. She hit a three-pointer, then two free throws. The Americans were on their way to another victory.

The American women then beat Korea and Japan. But the wins did not lighten the mood around their locker room. "It isn't a test when you play short people," said Edwards, referring to the height advantage the Americans had over the Japanese team.[8] The American women continued to put pressure on themselves. Even after beating Australia for the second time and advancing to the gold medal game, they were still not in a mood to celebrate. "It's still unfinished business," said guard Dawn Staley.[9]

Their opponent, Brazil, had beaten the Americans for the gold medal at the 1994 World Championships. The 110–97 loss to the Brazilians

Swoopes (far right) celebrates with her U.S. teammates after winning the gold at the 1996 Olympics in Atlanta.

had left a bad taste for the American women. When they won, the Brazilians had laughed and danced on the court and "maybe rubbed it in a little bit," said VanDerveer.[10] The Americans had to watch them continue to celebrate when they shared a bus after the game. "I wanted to get back and beat them," VanDerveer said.[11]

Now the Americans were ready. They led 57–46 at the half, and increased their lead in the second half.

One lasting image from the game was of Ruth Bolton stealing the ball from the Brazilians with about eleven minutes left. She rolled on the floor and fired a pass from her knees to Sheryl Swoopes for a basket.

Another lasting image was of Sheryl Swoopes knocking away a jump shot attempt on Brazil's next possession.

Finally, the Americans were able to celebrate with high fives and hugs and a victory lap around the court following their 111–87 win. Mission accomplished. And there was more good news. Two women's professional basketball leagues would be starting in America. The next stop for Sheryl Swoopes and many of her Olympic teammates would be the Women's National Basketball Association (WNBA).

Chapter 6

The Road Back

It was supposed to be "Swoopes—as in hoops." Instead, it was "Coop—as in MVP." And Sheryl Swoopes was missing in action.

Cynthia Cooper took "Sheryl Swoopes's team" and made it her own. And while the five-foot ten-inch guard was leading the Houston Comets, she became one of the WNBA's top players. Where was Sheryl Swoopes? At home, out of condition, and working hard to get back in shape.

Swoopes, the six-foot forward-guard, had a unique name and unique basketball talents. But those talents would not be put to the test at the professional level right away. She had stayed home to play the role of mom.

Swoopes's signing with the Comets in 1997 had made headlines in Houston: "Texas Girl Comes Home." She was fresh off her gold medal triumph at the Olympics. Everything was going her way. She was at the center of a marketing campaign to sell the new professional women's basketball league. "Swoopes—as in hoops" became a common phrase used in celebrating Sheryl Swoopes's ability.

But now Cynthia Cooper had taken her place and Swoopes was no longer the center of attention. Cooper was leading the Comets in just about every offensive category. While running the show in Houston, Cooper was also in the running for the league's Most Valuable Player award.

Sheryl Swoopes, meanwhile, was working hard to get back into shape. She was playing full-court, five-on-five basketball games. She was running. She was lifting weights. All the while, she was sweating off excess pounds. Swoopes might have taken the year off to spend more time with her new baby. But she missed basketball. She missed the action. She also felt she had a responsibility. The league had counted on her. The Comets had counted on her. Could she do it? Could she get back into shape in time to help the Comets make a bid for the WNBA Championship?

Despite Cynthia Cooper's best efforts, the

Comets were still trying to overtake the New York Liberty in their battle for first place in the Eastern Conference. Winning the WNBA Championship was not guaranteed for Houston. The Comets first had to figure out how to beat New York. They had lost all three games they had played against the Liberty.

As the runaway leader in the East in the first half of the season, the Liberty team was almost certain to gain a playoff berth. The same was not true of the Comets.

No one knew what to expect when Sheryl Swoopes finally joined the Comets late in the season. Swoopes herself was even unsure of what she would be able to do. In her first game in the WNBA, she played only five minutes. She touched the ball only once and almost lost it. She played eight minutes in the second game. And three in the third. Total minutes played: 16. Total shots taken: 2. Total points: 0.

Finally, a breakout game came in her fourth game, against Utah. Then she had another good game against Charlotte. "She has definitely given us a boost and given us a different offensive and defensive look," Cynthia Cooper said of her new teammate.[1]

Though not at her best, Swoopes was starting to

Lisa Leslie, Rebecca Lobo, and Sheryl Swoopes (left to right) turned pro by joining the newly-formed WNBA in 1996.

round into form. "If I had to say, I'd say I was 70 percent," she said.[2] It was still better than most players. After going scoreless in her first three games, she had scored a total of 38 in her next two. "I guess it's the competitor in me," Swoopes said. "I don't want to sit back and watch my team hopefully go to the championship. I wouldn't feel I was part of it."[3]

On the way to the championship, a roadblock appeared. The detour sign read: New York. The Liberty was still the team to beat for the Comets.

This was the same New York team that had beaten the Comets three times in a row earlier in the season—twice on their home court.

Despite struggling in the second half of the season, the Liberty still held first place in the Eastern Division. Now the Comets were going to New York to battle them for the division lead.

Madison Square Garden was the site of the big game. The arena was filled with nearly seventeen thousand five hundred screaming fans—the third largest crowd for a women's professional basketball game in North America. There was pressure to win on the road in front of the hostile New York fans. There was further pressure to secure first place and point the Comets toward the playoffs. Last, but certainly not least, there was pressure to beat a team

FACT

It's just before game time and guess what Sheryl Swoopes is doing in the locker room? Usually, she is listening to R&B music, drinking a soda, and eating a chocolate bar. That is normally the routine she follows, according to the Houston Comets' media guide.

that had seemingly held a jinx over them. It could be easy for a team to lose its confidence in these circumstances.

This would not happen to the Comets and Sheryl Swoopes. She looked forward to playing against Liberty superstar Rebecca Lobo. "This game and LA were the two teams I was really looking forward to playing this season," Swoopes said. "A lot of that had to do with the fact that Rebecca and Lisa [Leslie of Los Angeles] were my Olympic teammates."[4]

Sheryl Swoopes made her first appearance in the game with just over three minutes gone. The Liberty were leading, 4–2. Swoopes scored a basket and then scored again to spark a 13–1 run. When Swoopes walked off the court with her teammates at halftime, the Comets held a 28–22 lead.

The Liberty rallied in the second half to tie the score at 32. Tammy Jackson's basket gave the Comets the lead again with 15:55 remaining. The Comets scored 10 straight points to take a 42–32 lead. Swoopes capped the run with a free throw and then showed the defensive skills that had made her a star in college and the Olympics. When the Liberty's Vickie Johnson went up for a shot, Swoopes leaped in front to block it.

Swoopes, Cooper, and Tina Thompson combined for 13 straight Houston points as the Comets

Rebecca Lobo and Sheryl Swoopes pose with WNBA jerseys in an effort to promote the new league in October 1996, nearly a year before the first scheduled game.

pulled away to a 70–55 win. Those three players combined for 44 points in Houston's win.

Welcome to first place, Comets! Now they were the team in the driver's seat. But Coach Van Chancellor was still nervous. "The last time we were in the driver's seat, we just drove right out of the parking lot of the [Charlotte] Coliseum." The Comets had lost that game 80-71 despite a 20-point performance by Sheryl Swoopes.

The Comets still had a week left in the regular season. But the playoffs were within their grasp now. "Today's win gives us confidence that we can play with them and beat them," said Swoopes, who scored 11 points in just 23 minutes. "Especially on their home court."[5]

One week later, the Comets were celebrating. They were the Eastern Conference champions. They had finished the season with a good run to edge out the Liberty for the conference title. They also had the best record in the WNBA at 18–10.

Sheryl Swoopes had played an important part in the Comets' late-season surge. She gave the team another scoring threat to take the pressure off Cynthia Cooper. "Obviously, Cooper is their number one," said Rebecca Lobo. "And Swoopes is an added dimension."[6]

In the playoffs, the Comets could not be stopped.

They beat Charlotte and archrival New York—for the second time in two weeks—to win the first-ever WNBA Championship.

Sheryl Swoopes did not score any points in the playoffs. But she had made a major impact on the Comets' season while only playing a few weeks. One could only imagine what she would do playing an entire season from start to finish.

Chapter 7

Picking Up Speed

Wow—what happened? Practice had stopped for the Houston Comets. The gym was suddenly silent. The team trainer was bending over a fallen figure. Sheryl Swoopes was down on the court. She was in trouble. The faces of the players were grim as they watched Swoopes struggle to breathe.

This was the shocking scene that greeted Comets Coach Van Chancellor as he walked into the gym. "If you thought I panicked, yeah, you were right," he said. "If you thought it worried me to death, you were right."[1]

It had been just another normal practice day during the 1998 season, until Swoopes had collapsed on the court. She was sweating and she felt sick—too sick to get back on her feet.

Team trainer Michelle Leget had rushed to her side. Luckily, Swoopes never fully lost consciousness. "I believe she could still hear me. As long as we talked to her and kept her calm, it was all right," Leget said.[2]

Swoopes was rushed to a hospital for observation and testing. Meanwhile, Cynthia Cooper and Tina Thompson gathered the Comets players together in a circle on the basketball court to think positive thoughts for their fallen teammate. Several of them went to the hospital to keep watch.

"It's scary and difficult when you see a fellow teammate go down and you don't know exactly what's wrong," Coach Van Chancellor said. "You're worried and you're scared, and it could be anybody."[3]

Preparations for a game with the Sacramento Monarchs the following night were obviously no longer the main priority for the Comets. "That seems to be a million miles away," said the coach.[4]

Finally, relief. The diagnosis for Swoopes was dehydration—not enough fluids in the body. She would be fine after a night in the hospital. It had been an emotional, gut-wrenching day for the Comets. But it had been a unifying day as well. The next night, despite missing Swoopes's usually high point production, the Comets beat Sacramento. "We sent this one out to Sheryl," said Cynthia Cooper, who scored a season-high 34 points against the Monarchs. "We want her to get well."[5]

This feeling of team togetherness was far different than the atmosphere that had surrounded the Comets before the start of the season. Then it did not seem like it was all for one and one for all.

There had been rumors of trouble between Swoopes and Cooper. Each wanted to be No. 1 and they did not get along, according to sports writers. Confirmed one WNBA insider, "They're crowding each other on that team. It's about sponsorship dollars from the same sponsors. . . and it's also about which one gets to be Michael Jordan."[6]

When Sheryl Swoopes missed both the morning and evening practices one day without contacting the team, the rumors became stronger. The next day, Swoopes came in for a meeting with Coach Van Chancellor. Afterward the coach said, "Sheryl missed practice because she was concerned about some things and we just had to work it out."[7]

Coach Van Chancellor would not go into detail about Sheryl Swoopes's "concerns." But later in the season, addressing rumors of the friction between Swoopes and Cooper, Chancellor did say, "Every team goes through it sometimes; it just doesn't get into the press. It's no big deal."[8]

Swoopes came back to the team, apparently satisfied with her role on the Comets. "Since I've been here, Cynthia and I have sat down and talked," Swoopes said. "A lot of people thought there would be problems but I think Cynthia and I complement each other. I hope we can win four or five championships together."[9]

They were now putting their focus on the team—and what a team they had! Cooper and Swoopes were not the only stars. Thompson, a high-scoring forward, had the ability to take over a game. The rest of the Comets featured such bright talents as Kim Perrot, Monica Lamb, Janeth Arcain, and Yolanda Moore. New York Liberty coach Nancy Darsch called the Comets "an awesome team."[10] But did this "awesome" team have room for two superstars, or even more?

It appeared so on opening day when the Comets crushed the Liberty, 74–62, in a rematch of the 1997 WNBA finalists. Swoopes and Cooper looked like the perfect fit, combining for 24 of the Comets' first 25 points and 46 altogether.

And the beat went on. After 15 games of the 1998 season, the Comets were 14–1, including an impressive 25-point win over the Liberty. People were wondering if they could possibly go through the rest of the season without a loss. "I don't think there's any way," said Coach Van Chancellor, citing a tough road schedule and games against such strong teams as Phoenix, New York, Los Angeles, and Charlotte.[11]

The Comets had not missed a beat despite jumping from the Eastern Conference to the Western Conference in 1998 due to expansion. (The WNBA

FACT

Some of Sheryl Swoopes's favorite things:

Sport to play (other than basketball): Volleyball

Sport to watch (other than basketball): Football, volleyball

Hobbies: Playing video games and shooting pool

Athlete: Michael Jordan

Actress: Halle Berry

Actor: Denzel Washington

Singer: Whitney Houston

Food: Mexican

Ice Cream: Pralines 'n Cream

City: New York

Books: Romance novels

had added new franchises in Washington and Detroit.) Playing from the start of the season, Swoopes was starting to feel more a part of the team. She came into training camp trim and fit, having shed nearly fifty pounds over the summer. She was back to her college playing weight of 148 pounds.

She was quicker, more like the Sheryl Swoopes who had led Texas Tech to the national title and helped the United States win a gold medal at the Olympics. She was one of the Comets' hardest working players. In practices she went all out. She played as if she was trying to make up for lost time—which, of course, she was. It seemed as if no one could stop her determined bid to regain her superstar status. Not even a leg injury could keep her out of the lineup.

Swoopes still was not feeling her best when she finally returned to action following her scare with dehydration. But she desperately wanted to play, despite a tough stretch of four games in six nights. Utah would be a tough test, not only for the still-weakened Swoopes but for the Comets as a team. In their last meeting, the Comets had needed double overtime to beat the Starzz, who featured seven-foot two-inch center Margo Dydek.

Once again, the Starzz were giving the Comets problems. They led 51–40 early in the second half.

Then Sheryl Swoopes got busy. She scored 10 points in a 19–2 run, helping Houston take a 59–53 lead. One of her baskets was in classic Swoopes style. She stole the ball from Utah's Olympia Scott. Then she dribbled the length of the court for a layup.

Although Swoopes was admittedly weak from her recent illness, it certainly did not look that way. "I was very tired, fatigued and tried not to think about it when I got out there," she said.[12] Amazingly, she managed to play 31 minutes and score 18 points as the Comets beat the Starzz, 72–68. "She's back and playing like a hoss," said the coach, mangling the word "horse."[13]

The Comets were playing like a well-oiled machine. By the end of the season, they had lost only three times in thirty games. At 27–3 they had far and away the best regular season record in the WNBA. Finally, the Swoopes-Cooper controversy had been put to rest. "All the rumors I heard about problems between Sheryl and Cynthia didn't materialize," said Coach Van Chancellor. "We play well together as a team, and they have complemented each other."[14]

Cooper and Swoopes gave the Comets a dynamic duo. Cooper led the league in scoring with a 22.7 average. Swoopes, meanwhile, put together a splendid all-around season. She averaged 15.6

Coach Van Chancellor is drenched with champagne by Sheryl Swoopes as the Houston Comets celebrate another championship.

points a game, sixth in the league. She was also one of the top defensive players in the WNBA. Her average of 2.48 steals a game ranked third. She was also usually one of the Comets' top rebounders. It was on to the playoffs.

The Comets faced the Charlotte Sting in the opening round. With their spectacular record, the Comets seemed to be almost invincible. But they took nothing for granted. The regular season was history. This was playoff time, featuring the four best teams in the league.

FACT

Sheryl Swoopes will have a hard time forgetting the 2000 season. So will others who watched her play basketball. Some highlights for her that year:

- Member of the WNBA champion Houston Comets.
- Member of the gold medal winning team at the Summer Olympics in Australia.
- WNBA Most Valuable Player.
- WNBA Defensive Player of the Year.
- League's leading vote getter (for the second time) at the WNBA All-Star Game.
- Named to the All-WNBA First Team (for the third time).

Winning a league championship more than once in a row is one of the most difficult things to do in professional sports. "Any time you're the defending champion in anything, you know other teams are going to be out to beat you, and more than likely, they'll have better games against you," said Swoopes.[15]

Although the Comets rarely lost, the season had taken its toll. Sheryl Swoopes and Cynthia Cooper both suffered from sore knees. Kim Perrot had a sprained ankle. Even with their injuries, the Houston players soundly beat the Charlotte Sting, 85–71, in Game 1 at Charlotte. Cooper scored 27 points. Swoopes had 17 points and 8 rebounds. Perrot played 38 minutes and directed Houston's offense.

The Comets' locker room after the game looked like a hospital ward. Swoopes and Cooper had ice bags on their sore knees. Perrot wore an ice bag on her ankle. "We would love to go back home and close it out in two games," said Sheryl Swoopes. "That will give us a little more time to rest [for the finals]. I can heal. Cynthia can heal. Kim can heal. The entire team can heal."[16]

Two days later in Game 2, the injuries did not seem to bother the Comets at all. Sheryl Swoopes scored 14 points as the Comets took a 45–34 lead at the half. Cynthia Cooper took over in the second half, and Swoopes finished with a career-high 13 rebounds. The result was a 77–61 win for the Comets and a place in the WNBA Finals. Their next opponent was the Phoenix Mercury, a team that had handed the Comets one of their three losses during the regular season.

Swoopes was on a mission. When the Comets won the championship the year before, she had not scored a single point in the playoffs. "Not only do I have to prove something to the fans, but there's something that I want to prove to myself," she said.[17]

But she would not be proving anything in the opening game against Phoenix. She made only 3 of 14 shots and missed a basket with 2.6 seconds left that could have tied the game. The underdog Mercury pulled off a 51–54 victory with the help of a late shot by Jennifer Gillom.

The series moved to Houston for the second game and, if necessary, a third. But with the Mercury holding a 62–50 lead with less than eight minutes left in Game 2, it did not look like there would be a Game 3. The Mercury were on their way to a second straight victory over the Comets and one of the biggest upsets in the WNBA's short history. Fans who had watched their beloved Comets all season sat in stunned disbelief at the Compaq

Center. Their "invincible" team appeared on its way to losing the championship.

Then the Comets suddenly came to life, outscoring the Mercury 13–2. In the middle of the rally were none other than Sheryl Swoopes and Cynthia Cooper. During one big play, Swoopes blocked a shot and set up a fast break basket for Cooper. On another play Cooper returned the favor with a feed to Swoopes for a basket. Both plays helped the Comets pull within one point. The score was now 62–61.

The game went into overtime tied at 66. It was time for Swoopes to swing into action. She stole a pass and set up a basket for Cooper. Then with the Comets clinging to a 70–69 lead, Swoopes connected from the top of the free-throw circle. The Comets now held a three-point lead. Cooper made two free throws and Swoopes grabbed two key rebounds in the closing seconds. The Comets pulled out a heart-stopping 74–69 victory to stay alive in the WNBA Finals.

"When we got down about 10 points, the only people who believed we could come back were our fans and us," Swoopes said. "We always believed we could win this game. It never crossed my mind that we weren't going to win."[18]

One more victory and the Comets would repeat as WNBA champions. But with less than eight minutes left in the final game, the Comets were struggling to hold on to the lead. The score was 62–61 with more than seven minutes to go. There was still plenty of time for anything to happen. Then Sheryl Swoopes happened.

With 7:22 left, she made two free throws.

At 6:41, she set up Arcain with a razor-sharp pass for a layup.

At 6:03, she scored.

At 3:05, with Houston clinging to a 71–67 lead, she knocked down a teammate to get to the basket and block a shot by the Mercury's Michele Timms. It was one of the most spectacular rejected shots of the playoffs.

Sheryl Swoopes was not finished. With 1:05 left, she made two free throws after she was fouled while rebounding. The result was an 80–71 victory for the Comets. They had won their second straight championship in a dramatic turnaround for Sheryl Swoopes.

"I feel like I contributed a lot more this year than I did last year," she said.[19] A blizzard of red and blue confetti, courtesy of the sellout crowd of some sixteen thousand people at the Compaq Center, blanketed the court.

Cynthia Cooper won the playoff MVP award, as expected. Sheryl Swoopes won something more important. She had gained self-respect and the respect of others around the league.

Chapter 8

In a League of Her Own

It is the WNBA's third season in 1999. It is also game time and the starting lineups are introduced.

"Number twenty-two. . . SHERRRYLLLLL SWOOOOPES!" the announcer says, deliberately drawing out the name in dramatic tones.

The crowd responds: "SWOOOOOOOOOPES!"

Just like in her college days, this crowd reaction has become a ritual in the pros. Sheryl Swoopes looks over to the second row courtside seats at the Compaq Center in Houston where her biggest fans are sitting: her little boy, Jordan (named after Michael Jordan), and her mother, Louise. Jordan is wearing a basketball uniform with his mother's number on it. He smiles and raises his arms when he sees his mom.

The game begins. Swoopes steals a pass and races the length of the court for an easy layup. The crowd roars its approval. Speed is one of Sheryl Swoopes's biggest assets. She is probably as fast as anyone in the WNBA going from one end of the court to the other.

"That's the [most fun] part of the game to me. . . getting out on the fast break and running the floor," she says. She also loves getting the crowd into the play. "The fans really get into the fast break."[1]

Although she has played all positions, Swoopes's specialty is small forward. It is an all-around position that requires speed and agility, good defense, and accurate outside shooting ability. She does it all. And now in her third year in the WNBA, Swoopes was starting to fulfill her potential as a pro.

Swoopes had always been a fan favorite. But even she was amazed at her own popularity now. When Nike said it wanted to start a line of sneakers in her name, she "was speechless. I cried. I bawled. At first I thought they were joking. I don't even know what I thought. I was just out of it. I thought I was dreaming."[2]

Even though she has gained fame and fortune as a professional basketball player, she has not lost her sense of appreciation. It makes her feel good to see a

Sheryl Swoopes applauds as President Clinton holds up a Houston Comets jersey.

fan's face light up when she gives out an autograph or simply shakes hands. She was touched deeply once when a fan asked her for a pair of autographed sneakers. The fan was wheelchair-bound, without legs.

Sheryl Swoopes is always thinking of others. She takes time out of her busy schedule to do charity work. She has served as the spokesperson for RSV, a dangerous respiratory virus that affects babies and children under the age of two.

She also takes her responsibilities as a role model seriously. "I consider it a huge responsibility for me to do anything in my power to promote the game and not just basketball, but women's sports," she says.[3]

She was certainly doing that during the 1999 season. One night at the Compaq Center, an eleven-year-old girl wearing a Sheryl Swoopes jersey was watching Swoopes in person for the first time. What did she like about Swoopes? The girl said she loved to watch her pull down rebounds and dribble the length of the court to score a basket. On this night, the young fan was not disappointed. On one play, Swoopes took a bounce pass on a fast break and leaped toward the basket. She scored on her signature finger-roll shot.

There is something else the young fan liked

about Swoopes. She did not pout or curse when she played. And she did not show up the other team in any way. Usually, Sheryl Swoopes limited her on-the-court celebrations with teammates to a quick handclap or high five.

Swoopes's game had improved considerably in her third season. She was starting to contribute more than ever in her pro career. But it had not been an easy road for Swoopes. She tried to balance her responsibilities as a mother and a basketball player. "The most difficult part is traveling and being a mom, not being able to take my son with me a lot of times," she said.[4] When she could, she had her son and her mother traveling with her on road trips. Louise Swoopes was Jordan's second mom.

Swoopes had improved her game. Meanwhile, the WNBA had increased the number of its teams and continued to draw good crowds league-wide. The league had started with eight teams in 1997. By 1999, the WNBA had expanded to ten teams. There were four more teams scheduled to join the following year, all of them in NBA cities.

The 1999 season not only featured expansion, but a historic event—the WNBA's first All-Star Game. It was played in front of a sellout crowd at Madison Square Garden in New York. It was also broadcast to 125 countries in twenty languages. Sheryl Swoopes and Cynthia Cooper played for the West team that beat the East, 79–61. Then they hurried back to their Houston team to continue league play in the second half of the season.

They could not wait. The Comets had been one of the top teams in the WNBA before the All-Star Game. After the midseason break, it was business as usual for the Comets. But no one was handing them the league championship just yet.

Most everyone agreed it would be tough for the Comets to win a third straight title because of the WNBA's overall strength. When the rival American Basketball League folded, many of its top players joined the WNBA. The additional players

FACT

When the Houston Comets won the WNBA championship in 2000, they became only the fifth team in professional sports to win as many as four straight titles. The others and their strings:

Boston Celtics, seven straight (1960–66)

New York Yankees, five straight (1949–1953)

Montreal Canadiens, five straight (1956–60)

New York Islanders, four straight (1979–83)

created a more balanced league. It did not appear that any one team would dominate—not even the defending champions. The Comets also had another, more serious, problem: their inspirational point guard, Kim Perrot, was battling cancer. She was unable to play. WNBA fans wondered if her absence would upset the chemistry of the Comets, particularly in the playoffs.

There was no question the Comets were headed for the postseason. But could they win the title again? Only three other professional basketball teams had won as many as three straight championships. The Minneapolis Lakers, Boston Celtics, and Chicago Bulls, in the NBA, had all done it. The Comets hardly looked like any of them when they lost by 15 points to the Los Angeles Sparks in their playoff opener. "I'm not so much disappointed that we lost, but in the way we lost," Swoopes said. "We weren't very aggressive. It seemed like we just didn't want to play, for whatever reason."[5] Few teams gave the Comets as much trouble as the Sparks, who had handed the defending champions two of their six regular-season losses. And now one more loss and the Comets would be out of the playoffs.

The playoff loss was not the only thing that bothered the Comets. Kim Perrot had lost her battle with cancer. Now the team was in the midst of mourning.

With teammate and close friend Sheryl Swoopes sitting beside her, Kim Perrot waves to the crowd during a game in July 1999. Perrot had been diagnosed with cancer earlier that year.

They were also never more determined as they returned to Houston for Game 2 of the series and, hopefully, a Game 3. Their mission was to win a championship for Kim Perrot.

It was obviously on the minds of all the Houston players, particularly Cynthia Cooper, who was Perrot's closest friend. When Cooper sank a three-point shot in Game 2, she held an index finger and a clenched fist over her head to make a "10," Perrot's number. The Comets won the game easily, then finished off the Sparks in Game 3. Swoopes and Cooper each scored 23 points. The Comets were

FACT

During the 2000 WNBA playoffs, Sheryl Swoopes showed why she was considered the best all-around player in women's basketball. She made an impact in just about every facet of the game, finishing no lower than ninth in six categories:

Ranked first in points per game 20.7

Ranked first in steals per game 2.81

Ranked fifth in minutes per game 35.2

Ranked eighth in assists per game 3.8

Ranked eighth in field goal percentage . . .506

Ranked ninth in blocks per game 1.06

now in the WNBA Finals for the third straight year. For the second time, they would be playing against the New York Liberty.

The teams had become great rivals in the relatively short time that the league had been in existence. The finals opened in New York. The teams would play a second game and a third, if necessary, in Houston. With more than seventeen thousand New Yorkers screaming at Madison Square Garden, the Liberty would appear to have a big home court advantage. But there was no such thing in this fierce rivalry. After all, it featured some of the best-played basketball in the WNBA.

Despite the brilliant offensive talents of Cynthia Cooper, Sheryl Swoopes, and Tina Thompson— Houston's "Big Three"—the Comets were known more for their tough defense than their offense. It was the reason they had won two straight championships. Swoopes was the team leader on defense. She usually guarded the opposition's top scoring threat. In this case, that player was Crystal Robinson, a great three-point shooter. No problem. Swoopes held Robinson to 12 points in an inspired defensive effort by the Comets. She also scored 15 herself, contributing to a 73–60 win in Game 1.

Now the Comets had two chances at home to wrap up the title. They had won 14 straight games at the Compaq Center and appeared to be unbeatable at home. They were on their way to another victory in Game 2. They led by as many as 18 points in the first half. Only a total collapse could keep them from winning the game. Suddenly, the collapse started to take place.

The Liberty chipped away at the Comets' lead. Slowly, they began to catch up. With just a couple of seconds left, the Comets were holding on for dear life, leading by merely two points. But the Liberty still had a shot—and took it. Teresa Weatherspoon launched a three-pointer from behind midcourt, fifty-two feet away, just as the final buzzer sounded. The crowd held its breath as the shot swished through the net to give the Liberty an unbelievable 68–67 victory. The fans were shocked. So too were the Comets, who looked like they had the championship wrapped up.

There was nothing for the Comets to do but try again the following night. This time, both teams played brilliant defense. The Comets played it a little better, though, walking off with a 59–47 victory and their third straight title. There were signs in the stands at the Compaq Center remembering Perrot—one of them reading "3 for 10." The meaning was clear: a third championship for number 10 of the Comets who was gone but not forgotten.

Houston's Big Three (from left), Tina Thompson, Sheryl Swoopes, and Cynthia Cooper raise three WNBA trophies during a parade in 1999 honoring the three-time league champions.

As the seconds ticked down, the crowd chanted "three for Kim, three for Kim." In truth, Perrot—and her winning spirit—was never far from the players' hearts as they determinedly charged to the championship. "We said that Kim wasn't here physically but she was here in spirit," Swoopes said. "She will always be a part of the Comets."[6]

It was an especially satisfying victory for the Comets, who had been on an emotional roller coaster all season. The team had faced a series of personal problems. Along with losing Kim Perrot, Cynthia Cooper had also lost her mother to cancer. And Sheryl Swoopes and her husband had been divorced in the off-season. "It amazed me what we were able to accomplish after all we went through personally," Swoopes said.[7]

Along with the ultimate team prize, there were also individual awards to go around in Houston. Cynthia Cooper won her third straight scoring championship. Sheryl Swoopes repeated as the WNBA's Defensive Player of the Year. Coach Van Chancellor was Coach of the Year for the third time.

The Comets were a powerhouse. They were expected to contend for the championship again in 2000. And there was an unexpected development happening as the season got underway. Swoopes, who had been a defensive specialist and the No. 2

Sheryl Swoopes is all smiles as she accepts the WNBA's Most Valuable Player trophy in 2000.

scorer on the team behind Cooper, suddenly had taken over the scoring leadership. Playing against New York in a rematch of WNBA finalists on opening day, Swoopes scored 27 points as the Comets beat the Liberty 84–68. Amazingly, she had produced the game-high in points despite sitting out five minutes of the second half with leg cramps.

Swoopes continued to contribute MVP-type scoring totals as the season continued. She was at her peak again, having put her personal issues behind her. "The big difference this year is I'm relaxed," Swoopes said "I'm having fun. Everything I went through personally, that's done."[8] That was more than could be said of Cynthia Cooper. She suddenly found that she was no longer necessarily the Comets' "go-to" player. Sheryl Swoopes had taken some of the responsibility into her own hands. "It's not something I enjoy or even accept," Cooper said. "Coach Chancellor never actually came in and said it would happen. I was going through games and only getting five or six shots and I figured something had changed."[9]

Cynthia Cooper, the league's three-time scoring champion, had not totally lost her leadership role. But here is an example of how Swoopes was taking over games: The Comets were battling the Portland Fire in a grueling game that went into double overtime.

Swoopes took Cooper and Tina Thompson aside. She told them she did not want the game to go into another overtime. Swoopes then personally took charge, scoring 8 of her 29 points in the second overtime to win the game for the Comets.

Sheryl Swoopes was enjoying the best year of her WNBA career. She was getting the job done at both ends of the court. She was leading the league in both scoring and steals per game. She is shorter than most forwards in the league at six feet. Still, she was among the top ten in shots blocked. All the others in that category were six feet two inches or taller.

FACT

Starting with Sheryl Swoopes, the Houston Comets had three players among the top six in the voting for the WNBA's MVP in 2000. The results:

1. Sheryl Swoopes, Houston
2. Lisa Leslie, Los Angeles
3. Yolanda Griffith, Sacramento
4. Natalie Williams, Utah
5. Cynthia Cooper, Houston
6. Tina Thompson, Houston

Swoopes was rapidly gaining fans, not only in Houston but around the country. She was the leading vote getter for the All-Star Game for the second straight year. She had become the Comets' marquee player, but she was also a star throughout the league. "Even people who have never seen a WNBA game, if they know that Sheryl Swoopes is on NBC, then they get interested," said WNBA commissioner Val Ackerman.[10] There was also plenty of interest in the Comets as a team. Only four other major professional sports franchises had won as many as four straight championships. Now the Comets had a chance to join that select group.

With Sheryl Swoopes leading the way in the playoffs, the Comets completed sweeps of Sacramento and Los Angeles to advance to the finals. Their opponent, for the third time in four years, was the New York Liberty.

The Comets won the opener. One to go for the championship. But that was suddenly in question when Swoopes stepped on another player and injured her foot in the first half. She collapsed, sobbing in pain, and needed help to get off the court. She went to the locker room for treatment. She was determined to continue playing, no matter how much pain she was in. "This is the playoffs," she said. "This is a time when you have to suck it up and play through injuries and things like that."[11]

That she did. Cynthia Cooper hit a dramatic, game-tying three-pointer with 20 seconds left in the game. Then Sheryl Swoopes took over in overtime. Playing on a sprained ankle, she scored 7 of her team's 15 points. She finished with a finals-record 31 points. But, even better, the Comets won, 79–73. They had earned a fourth straight title. The Comets joined the Boston Celtics, New York Yankees, New York Islanders, and Montreal Canadiens as the only major professional sports teams to win four straight titles.

Sheryl Swoopes barely had any time to enjoy that triumph. She quickly rushed off to join the United States Olympic Team in Australia. Another Olympics brought another gold medal for Swoopes and the American women's team. But it would never get boring. "Every time I think it can't get better, it does," Swoopes said.[12]

When the individual awards were announced for the 2000 WNBA season, Swoopes was the league's scoring champion with a 20.7 average. She also picked up awards for Most Valuable Player and Defensive Player of the Year. She won the MVP award by a large margin over Lisa Leslie of the Los Angeles Sparks in the voting by sports writers and

FACT

Now you know why they called them "The Big Three." Sheryl Swoopes, Cynthia Cooper, and Tina Thompson were all named to All-WNBA teams after the Houston Comets won the league title in 2000. Swoopes, the leading vote-getter, and Cooper made the first team. Thompson was on the second team.

*A fourth championship trophy and a scream of joy as Sheryl Swoopes rides
in the celebration parade in Houston on August 29, 2000.*

broadcasters. Cynthia Cooper, who won the award in 1997 and 1998, finished fifth in what would be her final season. The league's all-time scoring leader would be retiring at the end of the year.

In accepting the MVP award, Swoopes began to cry. "I had said, if I won the MVP award this year, this is the one thing I wasn't going to do, cry. But I sit back and look at everything that I've accomplished throughout my career, this is definitely one that's very special to me."[13]

When the WNBA started in 1997, the league had hoped Sheryl Swoopes would take a leading role in its growth. She was the first player signed for the new league. Now, four years later, she was No. 1 again.

A knee injury sidelined Swoopes for the entire 2001 season. And with it went the Comets' hopes for a fifth straight title. But Swoopes was already working on her return to the WNBA. She vowed to put herself and the Comets back on top. Welcome, new season.

Chapter Notes

Chapter 1. Breaking Through

1. W. H. Stickney, Jr., "Cooper Steals Show As Comets Win," *Houston Chronicle*, August 8, 1997, sports, p. 1.

2. Sarah Hughes, "Swoopes Returns To Form," *Houston Chronicle*, August 13, 1997, sports, p. 3.

3. Ibid.

4. Ibid.

Chapter 2. Big-Time Dreams

1. Kimberly Goad, "Superstar Shoe Fits Team USA's Swoopes," *The Milwaukee Journal Sentinel*, February 4, 1996, sports, p. 7.

2. Erin Egan, "Olympic Big Shots Swooping Into Atlanta From Tumbleweeds To Awesome Deeds," *Sports Illustrated For Kids*, July 1, 1996, p. 62.

3. Mike Jones, "Score Her A Hero," *The Fort Worth Star-Telegram*, February 18, 1996, sports, p. 1.

4. Egan, p. 62.

5. Gerry Callahan, "Little Sister Driven To Prove Herself Against Her Older Brothers And Other Boys, Sheryl Swoopes Became Queen Of The Court," *Sports Illustrated*, July 19, 1996, p. 32.

6. Egan, p. 62.

7. Erin Davies, "Heir Jordan," *Texas Monthly*, June 1, 1999, p. 30.

8. Mike Jones, "Score Her A Hero," *The Fort Worth Star-Telegram*, February 18, 1996, sports, p. 1.

9. Callahan, p. 32.

10. Kimberly Goad, "Superstar Shoe Fits Team USA's Swoopes," *The Milwaukee Journal Sentinel*, February 4, 1996, sports, p. 7.

Chapter 3. Small-Town Girl, Big-Time Player

1. Earl Gustkey, "Big-Time Player, Small-Town Swoopes Stays Close To Home, Leads Texas Tech," *Los Angeles Times*, April 2, 1993, sports, p. 1.

2. Ibid.

3. Suzanne Haliburton, "Lady Longhorns Lose All American 'Homesick' Recruit," *Austin American-Statesman*, September 7, 1989, p. C1.

4. Gustkey, sports, p. 1

5. "Swoopes Credits South Plains College For Boosting Her Basketball Career," *JUCO Review*, October 1996, p. 53.

6. Ibid.

7. Cathy Harasta, "Spotlight Won't Blind Swoopes," *The Dallas Morning News*, February 24, 1993, p. 1B.

8. Rick Cantu, "Tech's Swoopes Sinks UT," *Austin American-Statesman*, January 12, 1992, p. E1.

Chapter 4. A Special Season

1. Tom Cooper, "Shaky Win For Cards Women," *The San Francisco Chronicle*, December 2, 1992, p. E1.

2. Joel Brown, "Swoopes Gets SPC Spotlight," *Lubbock Avalanche-Journal*, February 26, 1993, sports, p. 1.

3. Jonathan Feigen, "Texas Tech's Shooting Stars," *Houston Chronicle*, March 17, 1993, sports, p. 1.

4. Ibid.

5. Ibid.

6. Earl Gustkey, "Big-Time Player, Small-Town Swoopes Stays Close To Home, Leads Texas Tech," *Los Angeles Times*, April 2, 1993, sports, p. 1.

7. Ibid.

8. Ibid.

9. Janice Carr, "NCAA Women's Tournament," *The Orange County Register*, April 4, 1993, p. C15.

10. Joanne Korth, "Swoopes Records A Title for Raiders," *St. Petersburg Times*, April 5, 1993, p. 1C.

11. Vic Dorr, Jr., "47 by Swoopes Paces Red Raiders," *Richmond Times-Dispatch*, April 5, 1993, p. D1.

12. Peter Brewington, "Tech's Lone Star Didn't Do It Alone—But With 47 Points, Swoopes Made MVP Voting Easy," *USA Today*, April 5, 1993, sports, p. 1.

13. Ray Glass, "Lady Raiders Savor Moment," *Lubbock Avalanche-Journal*, April 5, 1993, p. 2C.

Chapter 5. Going for the Gold

1. Milton Kent, "Her Airness Even Winning Over Jordan," *The Baltimore Sun*, July 24, 1996, p. 7D.

2. Ibid.

3. Kimberly Goad, "Courting A Dream To Play Hoops In The '96 Olympics," *The Dallas Morning News*, January 21, 1996, p. 1E.

4. Kent, p. 7D.

5. Ibid.

6. Ibid.

7. Allan Johnson, "Swoopes Talks Hoops/We Shoot the Breeze With An Olympic Big Shot," *Chicago Tribune*, October 22, 1996, sports, p. 1.

8. Lynn Zinser, "U.S. Does An Inside Job To Defeat Japan," *The News Tribune* (Tacoma, Wash.), August 1, 1996, p. C5.

9. Bob Lipper, "Sub Staley Jump-Starts Americans," *Richmond Times-Dispatch*, August 3, 1996, p. D-1.

10. Tom Kensler, "U.S. Women Can't Wait For Revenge," *Denver Post*, August 3, 1996, p. CC-06.

11. Ibid.

Chapter 6. The Road Back

1. Neal Farmer, "Swoopes Continues To Get Her Game Back," *Houston Chronicle*, August 25, 1997, sports, p. 8.

2. Ibid.

3. Alan Hahn, "Swoopes, Like Her Team, Catching Up," *Newsday*, August 18, 1997, p. A35.

4. W. H. Stickney, Jr., "Comets Summary," *Houston Chronicle*, August 18, 1997, sports, p. 5.

5. Oscar Dixon, "Comets Improve Playoff Lot, Down Liberty, 70–55," *USA Today*, August 18, 1997, p. 10C.

6. Adam Zagoria, "Streaking Comets Surge Past Liberty," *The Star-Ledger* (Newark, N.J.), August 18, 1997, p. 37.

Chapter 7. Picking Up Speed

1. W. H. Stickney, Jr., "Swoopes Stable After Collapsing," *Houston Chronicle*, July 3, 1998, sports, p. 1.

2. Ibid.

3. Ibid.

4. Ibid.

5. Jody Goldstein, "Comets Show Real Team Effort," *Houston Chronicle*, July 4, 1998, sports, p. 4.

6. "Swoopes Takes Over As Comets Win Title," *The Tucson Citizen*, September 2, 1998, p. 3D.

7. Michael A. Lutz, The Associated Press, "Swoopes Returns With Apology," *The State Journal-Register* (Springfield, Ill.), June 11, 1998, sports, p. 39.

8. Tom Osborn, "Swoopes, There She Is." *San Antonio Express-News*, August 22, 1998, sports, p. 1C.

9. Lutz, sports, p. 39.

10. W. H. Stickney, Jr., "Comets Establish Standard," *Houston Chronicle*, July 15, 1998, sports, p. 1.

11. Ibid.

12. Brian McTaggart, "Swoopes Shakes Off Fatigue, Saves Victory," *Houston Chronicle*, July 12, 1998, sports, p. 4.

13. Ibid.

14. Valerie Lister, "Comets Set High Standards," *USA Today*, August 21, 1998, p. 3C.

15. Ibid.

16. Eddy Landreth, "Hobbling Comets Blast Past Sting," *Austin American-Statesman*, August 23, 1998, p. C1.

17. Valerie Lister, "Mercury Peak At Right Time," *USA Today*, August 27, 1998, p. 14C.

18. Jeff Metcalf, "In Prime Time, Swoopes Takes Lead Role," *The Arizona Republic*, August 30, 1998, p. C5.

19. Jeff Metcalf, "Three's A Crowd," *The Arizona Republic*, September 2, 1998, p. C1.

Chapter 8. In a League of Her Own

1. Scott Simonson, "WNBA Star Ready To Swoop In For Fourth Title," *Houston Chronicle*, August 17, 2000, p. 4.

2. Erin Davies, "Heir Jordan," *Texas Monthly*, June 1, 1999, p. 30.

3. "Basketball Star Embraces Chance To Make A Difference," *Houston Chronicle*, September 10, 2000, p. 9.

4. Bill O'Reilly and Robert Dornan, "O'Reilly TV Interview With WNBA Star Sheryl Swoopes," *Fox News: The O'Reilly Factor*, November 19, 1999.

5. W. H. Stickney, Jr., "Houston Comets Summary," *Houston Chronicle*, August 29, 1999, sports, p. 8.

6. Michael A. Lutz, The Associated Press, "Comets Win WNBA Title: '3 For Kim'," *Fort Lauderdale Sun-Sentinel*, September 6, 1999, p. 1C.

7. W. H. Stickney, Jr., "One For The Team," *Houston Chronicle*, May 23, 2000, sports, p. 5.

8. Oscar Dixon, "Swoopes Soars To Head Of Class," *USA Today*, June 20, 2000, p. 3C.

9. Jumoke R. Gamble, "Out Of This World Attention: Olympian Sheryl Swoopes Is The WNBA's Brightest Star," *Orlando Sentinel*, June 26, 2000, p. B1.

10. Ibid.

11. W.H. Stickney, Jr., "Swoopes Battles Back From Injury," *Houston Chronicle*, August 27, 2000, sports, p. 4.

12. "Basketball Star Embraces Chance To Make A Difference," *Houston Chronicle*, September 10, 2000, p. 9.

13. W. H. Stickney, Jr., "Swoopes Wows Them Over, Captures MVP Honors," *Houston Chronicle*, August 18, 2000, sports, p. 8.

Career Statistics

WNBA

Team	Year	GP	FG%	Reb.	Ast.	Stl.	Blk.	Pts.	Avg.
Houston	1997	9	.472	15	7	7	4	64	7.1
Houston	1998	29	.427	149	62	72	14	453	15.6
Houston	1999	32	.462	202	127	76	46	585	18.3
Houston	2000	31	.506	195	119	87	33	643	20.7
Houston	2001	INJURED-DID NOT PLAY							
Totals		101	.468	561	315	242	97	1745	17.3

GP—Games Played
FG%—Field Goal Percentage
Reb.—Rebounds
Ast.—Assists

Stl.—Steals
Blk.—Blocks
Pts.—Points Scored
Avg.—Points per Game

Where to Write
Sheryl Swoopes

Ms. Sheryl Swoopes
c/o The Houston Comets
Two Greenway Plaza, Suite 400
Houston, TX 77046-3865

On the Internet at:

The Official Web Site of the WNBA
<http://www.wnba.com>

The Official Web Site of the Houston Comets
<http://www.wnba.com/comets/>

Index

921 SWO
Rappoport, Ken
Sheryl Swoopes, star forward

29927